ARBORAMA

arbo-

From the Latin *arbor* meaning *tree*.

-orama

From the Greek *hórama* meaning *vision*.

ARBORAMA
The Marvelous World of Trees

Text and illustrations: Lisa Voisard

Layout and typesetting: Lisa Voisard
and Elżbieta Kownacka

American adaptation: Andrée Hallé

Translation from French: Jeffrey K. Butt
Science editor: Paul D. Henne
Editors: Aude Pidoux, Richard Harvell,
Angela Wade
Proofreader: Karin Waldhauser

Front cover: Redwood
Back cover: Leaves of the American beech
and sugar maple, fruit of the basswood
and common apple, flower of the chokecherry

ISBN: 978-3-907293-90-4
First Edition: 2023
Printed in China

Avenue des Acacias 7
CH-1006 Lausanne, Switzerland

HEL
VETIQ
www.helvetiq.com

HELVETIQ publishing has received a structural grant from
the Swiss Federal Office of Culture for the years 2021–2025.

With support from:

canton de vaud

Ville de Lausanne
Service des bibliothèques
& archives

Schweizerische Eidgenossenschaft
Confédération suisse
Confederazione Svizzera
Confederaziun svizra

Swiss Confederation

Federal Department of Home Affairs FDHA
Federal Office of Culture FOC

Lisa Voisard

ARBORAMA

The Marvelous World of Trees

Translated by Jeffrey K. Butt

North American Edition

Table of contents

2 Go on, take a good look around!

3 The life of trees

What are trees?

So big

The size of trees really set them apart from other plants. The largest can grow to 50, 150 or even more than 300 feet tall! Trees don't just grow up—they grow out, too! Anything taller than about 20 feet is considered a tree, while anything shorter is generally considered a shrub.

So strong

Wood is strong and resilient, which allows some trees to live for 100, 500 or even 4000 years! They're built to tolerate urban pollution and to survive storms, avalanches, droughts, and extreme temperatures.

So important

There are more than 60,000 species of trees in the world. Each one is ecologically beneficial to both humans and animals—they clean the air, provide wood and fruit, beautify our landscapes, and help keep the ecosystem working properly.

Treetop
Branches and twigs
Foliage (leaves)
Crown
Limbs
Trunk
Roots

Why do trees have leaves?

Leaves are a tree's lungs, allowing it to breathe. They catch the sun's light and convert it into the stored energy a tree needs to thrive.

Northern red oak leaf

What about flowers?

Flowers are a tree's reproductive organs. Flowers can be single or in clusters.

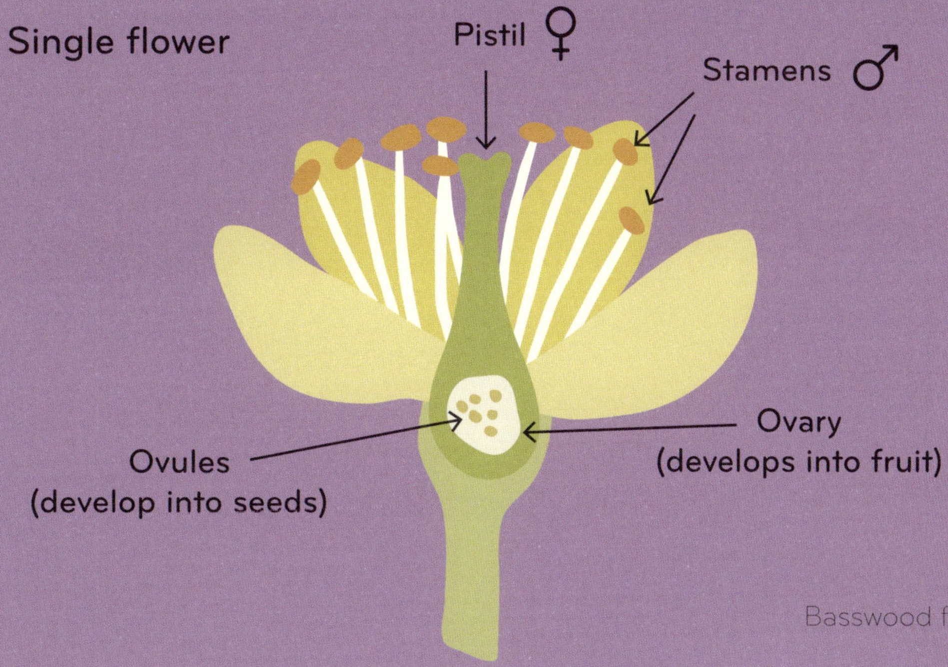

Basswood flower

Inflorescence (or cluster) of flowers

Catkins
of a trembling aspen

Flowers
from an Ohio buckeye

What does fruit do?

Once a flower is fertilized, it can turn into a fruit. The fruit contains seeds that will become new trees.

What are cones?

Cones work something like flowers. Pollen from male cones fertilizes female cones, which then produce seeds protected by scales.

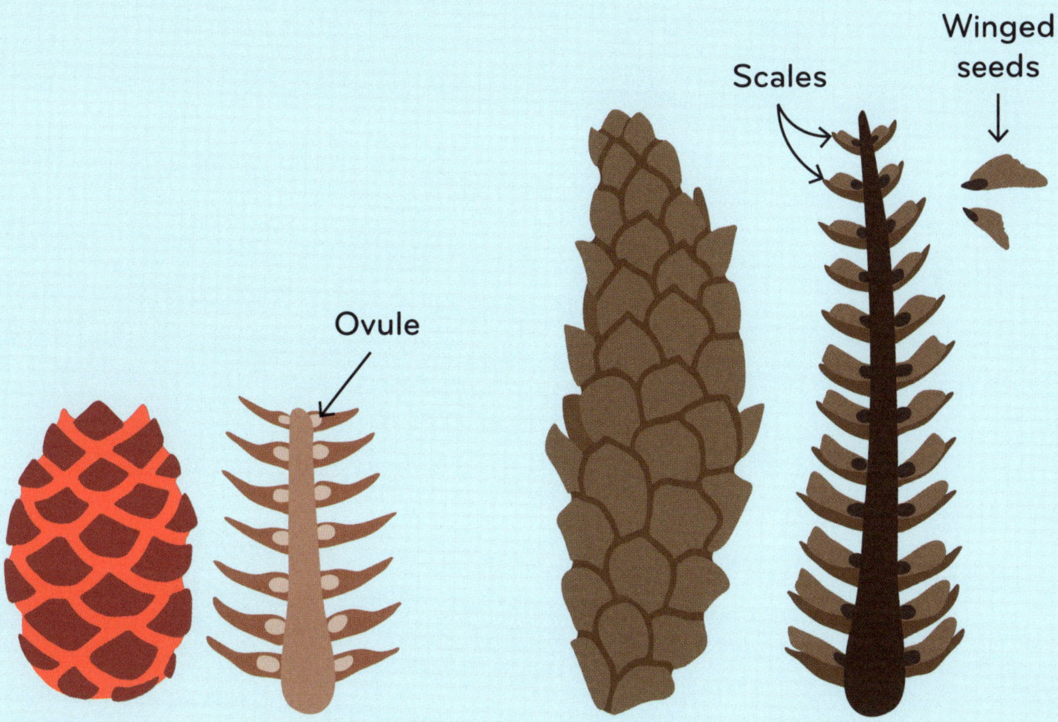

Young female cone

Mature female cone

Cone of an eastern white pine

Classifying trees

To help identify and categorize trees, here is a simple classification system.

Two groups

Broad-leaved trees

Broad-leaved trees have flat leaves that come in many different shapes and sizes. These include birch, oak, and maple trees.

Coniferous trees

Conifers have needles and cones, and include redwoods, firs, and spruces.

Six shapes

Round

Oval

Slender

Cone

Weeping

Umbrella

Three types of reproduction

Dioecious

Each tree has either male or female flowers, but never both. Examples include the weeping willow, white ash, and western yew.

Monoecious

Each individual has both male and female flowers. The black walnut, northern red oak, and eastern white pine are examples.

Hermaphroditic

Each specimen has flowers that are both male and female: the apple tree, Ohio buckeye, and southern magnolia, for example.

→ **For more information, go to page 191**

Three main habitats

Towns, cities, and parks

These trees are usually planted by humans. Their ability to tolerate pollution, cool down temperatures, and brighten up our surroundings make them worthy of our admiration.

Forests and countryside

Here, they like to grow in groups, creating underground root networks and providing food and shelter to animals.

Forests and mountains

Some trees happily grow at high altitudes, taking root on steep slopes and withstanding harsh weather conditions.

1

Portraits

Every tree is different! Some are exquisitely slim and slender, others sport a leafy crown, some appear ready for battle—with spiky needles, thorny fruit, serrated leaves, or pointy buds—and of course there are the flowery show-offs. No matter where they grow—cities, forests, mountains, or lowlands—trees come in a wide variety of shapes and colors.

American sycamore

p. 19

Basswood

p. 23

Black walnut

p. 29

Chokecherry

p. 33

Common apple tree

p. 37

Ginkgo
p. 43

Ohio buckeye
p. 49

Towns, cities, and parks

Southern magnolia
p. 53

Weeping willow
p. 57

American sycamore

Looking slick in the city

Group Broad-leaved	**Shape** Round, oval	**Reproduction** Monoecious	**Habitat** Towns, cities, and parks

American sycamores tolerate pollution and cool the air, so cities have them in abundance. The tree's Latin name is "Platanus," from the Greek "platanos," meaning "flat." Some speculate the tree's name has to do with the shape of its leaves—flat and broad.

Among the tree's more noteworthy—and fascinating—traits is its mottled bark, which looks like army fatigues or pieces of a jigsaw puzzle.

As fall turns into winter, the sycamore stands bare, revealing its thick branches and orb-like fruit dangling from a long peduncle, or stalk. The fruit lingers on the tree throughout winter and disperses the seeds in spring.

Lifespan
~250 years

Height
60 to 120 feet

Scientific name
Platanus occidentalis

A year in the life...

The American sycamore is a **deciduous** tree, dropping its leaves for the winter. It blooms in spring and its fruit remains on the tree during winter.

Spring Summer Fall Winter

Bark

Brown, beige, and gray, with patterned scales resembling a jigsaw puzzle or army fatigues.

Not to be confused with...

... the sugar maple, with more sharply indented leaves and veins branching out from the same point. It also has oppositely arranged buds. Sugar maple fruits are samaras, while those of the American sycamore are spherical.

Found

The American sycamore is native to eastern and central parts of the United States, extending into the mountains of northeastern Mexico and the most southern parts of Ontario and Quebec. The tree has been introduced into Europe.

Observation guide

Basswood

A loving healer

Group
Broad-leaved

Shape
Oval

Reproduction
Hermaphroditic

Habitat
Towns, cities, parks, and forests

A symbol of love and fidelity, the basswood is adorned with pretty, heart-shaped leaves. In spring, its crown quickly fills out and small, drooping flowers burst out everywhere, giving off a heavy, honey-like fragrance. During the summer, the basswood makes a great shade tree and helps cool the air.

Tea made from dried basswood flowers acts as a soothing sedative and helps relieve anxiety. And basswood honey is a tasty addition to any breakfast.

The tree's soft wood is perfect for woodworkers, who use it to make carvings, engravings, and even piano keys.

Lifespan
100 to 150 years

Height
75 to 130 feet

Scientific name
Tilia americana

A year in the life...

The basswood is a **deciduous** tree, shedding its leaves for the winter. The tree blooms in June or July after getting its new leaves.

Bark

Gray, with intersecting ridges.

Not to be confused with...

... the small-leaved linden, whose leaves are half as big (about 1.5 × 1.5 inches), with tiny, rust-colored hairs on the underside.

Found

The basswood is found throughout the northeastern United States, extending into southern Canada. It likes to grow alongside other broad-leaved trees, such as the sugar maple, oak, and American beech.

Observation guide

A greenfly gathering place

If you ever turn over a basswood leaf, you're likely to see little bunches of greenflies, or aphids. Ants and bees are attracted to their sugary poop, known as "honeydew." It's not uncommon for a car parked under a basswood to be covered in black spots, which are actually fungi growing on honeydew droplets from the tree above.

Black walnut

A carpenter's dream

Group
Broad-leaved

Shape
Round

Reproduction
Monoecious

Habitat
Towns, cities, and parks

The black walnut has many different uses: woodworkers sand the dark wood to reveal stunning patterns in the grain; naturopaths use the tree's leaves to treat itchy rashes; walnut ink—a natural dye used to stain furniture and textiles—is made from the fruit's flesh, or husk; and pressing the kernel, or walnut, produces a gorgeously scented oil. And if that was not enough, the walnut itself is edible and delicious!

Still, the black walnut has somewhat of a "toxic" presence... it excretes juglone, a poisonous compound that prevents other plants from growing near it.

Lifespan
~200 years

Height
80 to 125 feet

Scientific name
Juglans nigra

A year in the life...

The black walnut is a **deciduous** tree, shedding its leaves for the winter. It blooms in spring and its walnuts are harvested in fall.

Spring Summer Fall Winter

Bark

Dark brown with rounded, intersecting ridges.

Not to be confused with...

... the white ash, which has fewer, rounder leaflets and oppositely arranged buds. White ash fruits are samaras, while those of the black walnut are walnuts.

Found

The black walnut grows in central and eastern regions of the United States and southern Canada. It is also found in Europe.

Observation guide

Chokecherry

A summery start to spring

Group
Broad-leaved

Shape
Round

Reproduction
Hermaphroditic

Habitat
Towns, cities, and countryside

In spring, chokecherries are bee magnets—bees spend their days buzzing from one tree to another. There's such a commotion, you'd think each tree was a beehive! Caterpillars, beetles, small rodents, and birds love to feast on the cherries, but humans usually find them too bitter to eat—hence the name!

A chokecherry in bloom is truly a sight to behold! But the show is over before you know it, as the petals fall from the pretty spikes of flowers and the fruit begins to emerge.

In fall, chokecherry leaves go from green to a beautiful copper. Whatever the season, chokecherries are a riot of color!

Lifespan
~100 years

Height
3 to 20 feet

Scientific name
Prunus virginiana

A year in the life...

The chokecherry is a **deciduous** tree, dropping its leaves for the winter. It blooms in early summer, and the cherries are ripe just a few weeks later.

Bark

Gray to brown and streaky, peeling off in horizontal strips.

Not to be confused with...

... the juneberry, whose leaves are rounder. The fruits can resemble the juneberry's too, but have longer stems and can be violet or pink.

Found

The chokecherry grows throughout North America, except in the south and far north.

Observation guide

Common apple

Not so common after all...

Group Broad-leaved	**Shape** Round	**Reproduction** Hermaphroditic	**Habitat** Towns, cities, and countryside

Every spring, apple trees are cloaked in beautiful white to light pink flowers, which give way to the little round fruits that become crisp, delicious apples. Once harvested, apples can be stored in climate-controlled conditions, away from light, to be enjoyed months later!

There are no limits to an apple's culinary uses: preserves, pies, juice, cider, and vinegar! In fact, after bananas and citrus fruit, apples are the most commonly eaten fruit in the world.

On a symbolic level, apples evoke the temptation of Eve in the Garden of Eden, or the tale of *Snow White* by the Brothers Grimm. New York City is affectionately known as "The Big Apple," and the apple even turns up in Isaac Newton's theory of gravity, which he reputedly devised after seeing one fall from a tree!

Lifespan
~100 years

Height
10 to 15 feet

Scientific name
Malus domestica

A year in the life...

The apple tree is a **deciduous** tree, losing its leaves for the winter. It blooms in spring and the apples are harvested in fall.

Spring Summer Fall Winter

Bark

Grayish brown, sometimes tending toward purple, with scaly chips.

Not to be confused with...

... the pear tree, which has flowers that are completely white, and leaves that grow on a longer stalk.

Found

Apple trees grow throughout the world. The crabapple (*Malus coronaria*) is the only apple native to North America.

Observation guide

Thousands of varieties

North Americans eat apples more than any other fruit. Apples are also an important commodity throughout the world. There are more than 7500 varieties!

Gala
Red Delicious
Golden Delicious
Fuji

Ginkgo

A living fossil

Group
Broad-leaved

Shape
Oval, round, slender

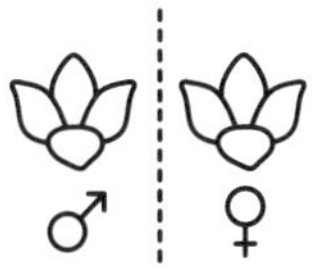

Reproduction
Dioecious

Habitat
Towns, cities, and parks

Native to southeastern China, the ginkgo can live to be more than 3000 years old. According to archaeologists and scientists, it is among the oldest living species of trees! In fact, the ginkgo was around when—and even before—dinosaurs walked the Earth. The famous British naturalist Charles Darwin named it a "living fossil."

"Ginkgo" means "silver apricot" in Chinese, a name that can probably be attributed to the tree's yellow ovules, which contain a nut used in traditional Asian cooking. The ginkgo is also called the "maidenhair" tree because its leaves resemble the fronds of the maidenhair fern. Its fan-shaped leaves make ginkgo truly unique.

The ginkgo is beautiful and tolerates pollution well, making it the perfect ornamental for urban settings.

Lifespan
+ 3000 years

Height
50 to 80 feet

Scientific name
Ginkgo biloba

A year in the life...

The ginkgo is a **deciduous** tree, shedding its leaves for the winter. Pollination occurs in spring.

Spring | Summer | Fall | Winter

Bark

Brown to light gray, rather smooth but cracking with age.

Shaped like no other!

The ginkgo leaf is totally unique, which is why it would be impossible to mistake it for any other tree!

Found

Ginkgos originated in southeastern China but are used ornamentally the world over.

Observation guide

When dinosaurs roamed...

The ginkgo is one of the oldest tree species still around today. Appearing some 270 million years ago, it stood alongside the dinosaurs! It might even have been on the menu for brachiosauruses and other large dinosaurs.

Ohio buckeye

A breathtaking bloomer

Group Broad-leaved	**Shape** Round, oval	**Reproduction** Hermaphroditic	**Habitat** Towns, cities, and parks

In springtime, park enthusiasts are treated to a buckeye bonanza, with magnificent clusters of pink-speckled, cream-colored flowers. The tree's leaves are made up of five to seven folioles (the leaflets that make up a compound leaf), which can grow to 6 inches or more!

In fall, children love to collect the bright, smooth nuts off the ground. Careful, though, because these nuts are poisonous—unlike chestnuts, which are edible! Although buckeyes are toxic to animals, some species of squirrel are able to eat them.

Tiny critters like leafhoppers and scale insects, despite their minuscule size, can defoliate an entire Ohio buckeye!

Lifespan
~80 years

Height
20 to 40 feet

Scientific name
Aesculus glabra

A year in the life...

The Ohio buckeye is a **deciduous** tree, losing its leaves for the winter. It blooms in spring and its fruit is ripe in fall.

Spring Summer Fall Winter

Bark

Gray turning dark brown, coarse and grooved, becoming scaly with age.

Not to be confused with...

... the American chestnut, which has simple (that is, not "compound") leaves. Its fruit—the chestnut—has little hairs at the top and comes in a spinier burr.

Found

The Ohio buckeye is found in eastern and central regions of the United States, extending into southern Canada. It has also been introduced into Europe.

Observation guide

Southern magnolia

Colossal blossoms

Group
Broad-leaved

Shape
Round, oval, or cone

Reproduction
Hermaphroditic

Habitat
Towns, cities, and parks

The southern magnolia is admired for the splendor of its white, fragrant flowers that can grow to 8 inches in diameter! Interestingly, this species keeps its flowers all summer long.

But what makes it truly special is that it is one of only two varieties of magnolia to keep its leaves throughout winter! The thick, evergreen leaves are dark green and glossy on top, with a downy, rust-colored underside.

Magnolias are among the most ancient plants on Earth. Just like with ginkgos, fossilized magnolia flowers have been discovered dating back to the time of the dinosaurs!

Lifespan
80 to 120 years

Height
60 to 90 feet

Scientific name
Magnolia grandiflora

A year in the life...

The southern magnolia is an **evergreen** tree, keeping its leaves all winter long.
It blooms in spring and throughout the summer.

Bark

Light brown to light gray.

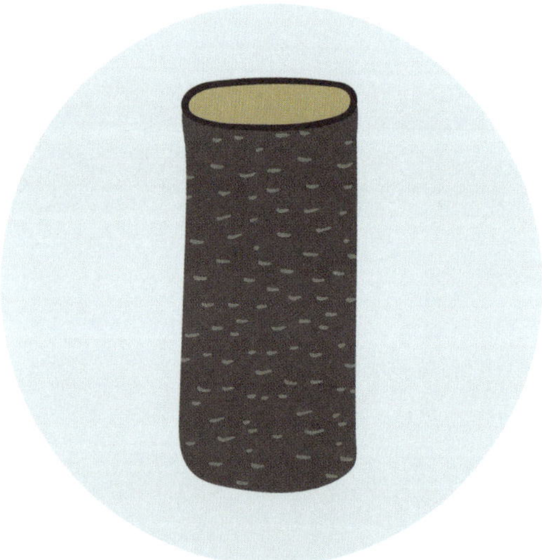

Not to be confused with...

... the tulip tree, whose flowers are also very big but shaped like tulips.

Found

The southern magnolia is native to the southeastern United States and has been widely planted for its flowers in warm regions around the world.

Observation guide

Weeping willow

The poet

Group
Broad-leaved

Shape
Weeping

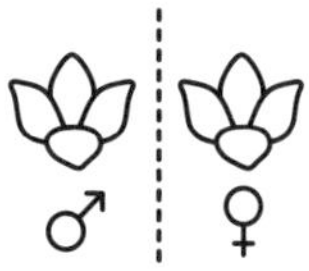

Reproduction
Dioecious

Habitat
Towns, cities, parks, and countryside

You might think a tree named "weeping willow," with water droplets streaming down its leaves like teardrops, would be an unhappy tree. But the name merely reflects the drooping nature of its branches, and the droplets... well, they're just condensation.

Native to China, the weeping willow makes a beautiful ornamental tree. With a preference for cool, wet roots, it grows happily near ponds and lakes.

Its leaves are among the first to appear in spring—long, slender, and bright green—as well as the last to go, falling in shades of yellow and brown. Countless painters and poets have drawn inspiration from the gracefulness of its branches, which seem to just dance in the wind. Weeping willows can make any landscape seem wistful, tranquil, and romantic.

Lifespan
~75 years

Height
30 to 50 feet

Scientific name
Salix babylonica

A year in the life...

The weeping willow is a **deciduous** tree, shedding its leaves for the winter. It blooms in spring.

Spring Summer Fall Winter

Bark

Light grayish brown, with a network of rather deep ridges.

Not to be confused with...

... the peachleaf willow, which has wider leaves and does not have a weeping form.

Found

The weeping willow is native to China but has been introduced into North America, Europe, Africa, and Australia.

Observation guide

American beech
p. 63

American elm
p. 71

American chestnut
p. 67

American hornbeam
p. 77

Gray alder
p. 87

Northern red oak
p. 91

Paper birch
p. 97

Eastern white pine
p. 83

Forests and countryside

Shagbark hickory
p. 101

Sugar maple
p. 105

Tamarack
p. 111

American beech

Simply majestic

Group Broad-leaved	**Shape** Round	**Reproduction** Monoecious	**Habitat** Forests and countryside

The America beech can be found in eastern North America. It is easily identifiable, with its smooth, gray bark and a pattern resembling eyes.

Quite remarkably, the beech's copper leaves fall and gather around the base of the tree before winter, wrapping the roots in a warm, protective blanket. But some leaves remain on the tree, clinging to its branches all winter long until they are pushed out by new leaves in spring—a phenomenon known as "marcescence."

Sometimes, the largest beeches have roots that look like elephants' feet!

Lifespan
200 to
400 years

Height
65 to 80 feet

Scientific name
Fagus grandifolia

A year in the life...

The American beech is a **deciduous** tree, shedding its leaves for the winter. It blooms in spring and its fruit is ripe in fall.

Spring

Summer

Fall

Winter

Bark

Silvery gray, smooth with gentle horizontal streaks.

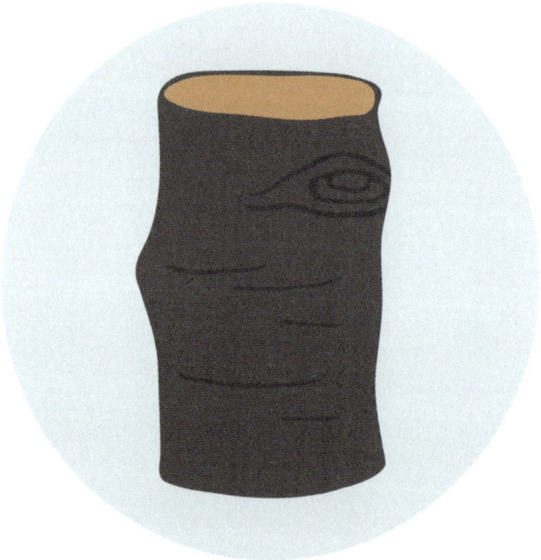

Not to be confused with...

... the American hornbeam, with double-toothed leaves that lack the little hairs found along the margin of the beech leaf.

Found

The American beech is the only beech native to North America. It can be found in central and eastern parts of the continent.

Observation guide

American chestnut

Ouch! That hurts!

Group
Broad-leaved

Shape
Round, oval

Reproduction
Monoecious

Habitat
Forests and countryside

In the past, the American chestnut was one of the most common trees in the northeastern United States and Appalachian Mountains, but over the last century a parasitic fungus called "chestnut blight" devastated the species. To keep it from disappearing altogether, researchers are trying to develop hybrids from Asian species of chestnut.

The tree is renowned for its fruit: the chestnuts that people love to gather in fall. But be careful if you find them! Chestnuts are encased in a spiny burr known as a cupule. After falling to the ground, these cupules open to reveal their fruit—to the delight of the deer and bears who love them! Chestnuts are high in calories and help these animals fatten up for the winter.

Lifespan
200 to 300 years

Height
50 to 75 feet

Scientific name
Castanea dentata

A year in the life...

The American chestnut is a **deciduous** tree: it drops its leaves for the winter. It blooms during the summer and its chestnuts are ready for harvest in fall.

Spring Summer Fall Winter

Bark

Gray and smooth in young trees, becoming furrowed with flat ridges as it ages.

Not to be confused with...

... the Ohio buckeye, which has a compound leaf. Its nut-like seed is round and smooth, and enclosed in a capsule that is less prickly than the American chestnut's.

Found

The range of the American chestnut is limited to eastern North America, extending as far north as southern Ontario and Quebec.

Observation guide

American elm

A perfectly imperfect leaf

Group Broad-leaved	**Shape** Umbrella, round	**Reproduction** Hermaphroditic	**Habitat** Forests and countryside

The American elm often has an umbrella-shaped canopy, but it can be round too. The easiest way to recognize this tree is by its leaves, which are asymmetric—a small lobe can be seen growing around the base of the stem, or petiole.

This tree is the first to the party! Already in winter, pretty bunches of flowers begin to appear, bursting out like a tiny display of fireworks. Once fertilized, the flowers become fruit—round samaras sheathed in winged, seed-spreading membranes.

In the 1970s, a fungus wiped out most mature trees, which were widely planted in towns and cities. Young elms can still be found in fields, near bodies of water and, less frequently, in urban settings.

Lifespan
~200 years

Height
40 to 60 feet

Scientific name
Ulmus americana

A year in the life...

The American elm is a **deciduous** tree, dropping its leaves for the winter. It blooms in late winter before its leaves come out. By spring, its fruit has already reached maturity.

Spring Summer Fall Winter

Bark

Gray, becoming fractured and frayed with age.

Not to be confused with...

... the American hornbeam, which has symmetric, double-toothed leaves.

Found

The American elm can be found all over North America, east of the Rocky Mountains.

Observation guide

Gone with the wind

The wind is responsible for spreading the American elm's abundant, winged seeds, which measure less than half an inch in diameter.

American hornbeam

The "musclewood" tree

Group
Broad-leaved

Shape
Oval, round

Reproduction
Monoecious

Habitat
Forests and countryside

The serrated leaves of the hornbeam are an attractive, bright, pale green. The leaves make a delicious snack for white-tailed deer.

The tree's vertically ridged bark is gray and quite smooth, while its pointy, reddish buds hug the branch. It is at home on lowlands, growing at elevations of up to 3200 feet.

The "musclewood" name comes from the fluting or ridges in the trunk and large branches, which give it a muscle-like appearance. Plus, hornbeam wood is as hard as rock, which is why the tree is sometimes also called "ironwood." It is used to make objects that have to be tough and sturdy, like tool handles.

Lifespan
~100 years

Height
20 to 35 feet

Scientific name
Carpinus caroliniana

A year in the life...

The American hornbeam is a **deciduous** tree, dropping its leaves for the winter. It blooms in spring and its fruit is mature in fall.

Spring Summer Fall Winter

Bark

Gray and rather smooth, with vertical ridges.

Not to be confused with...

... the American beech, whose leaves have smaller serrations, or "teeth."

Found

The American hornbeam is found throughout eastern North America, as far as west Texas.

Observation guide

Non-identical triplets!

The American hornbeam is often confused with the American beech and the American elm, but there are subtle differences in their leaves.

The leaf is
single-toothed
American beech

American elm
The leaf is
asymmetrical

Eastern white pine

Five-fingered fascicles

Group
Conifer

Shape
Cone,
irregularly shaped

Reproduction
Monoecious

Habitat
Forests, countryside,
and mountains

The eastern white pine has needles that can be up to 6 inches long and are grouped in fascicles, or bundles, of five. Long, drooping female cones start out green but become brown as they age. At maturity, they open up to release small, winged seeds. The bark of this handsome conifer is a rather dark grayish brown, and notched with broad ridges.

The eastern white pine has valuable lumber and was heavily logged during the 1800s. Conservation efforts have been hampered by the white pine weevil, a small insect that colonizes the top of the tree. Its larvae have a voracious appetite and in just a few weeks can destroy two- or three-years' worth of growth.

Lifespan
~450 years

Height
60 to 150 feet

Scientific name
Pinus strobus

A year in the life...

The eastern white pine is an **evergreen** tree, keeping its needles all year.

Pollination occurs in spring, and it takes two years for its cones to reach maturity.

Bark

Thin and smooth, turning dark grayish brown and developing broad ridges with age.

Not to be confused with...

... the red pine, whose needles are generally longer and bundled in pairs.

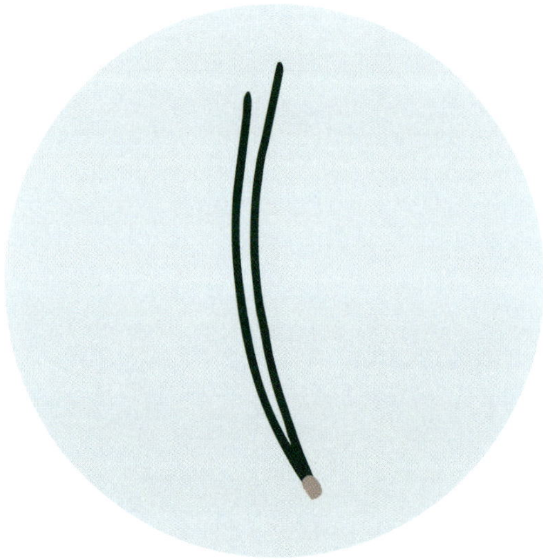

Found

The eastern white pine is found throughout eastern North America. It has been introduced into Europe.

Observation guide

Gray alder

The marshmate

Group
Broad-leaved

Shape
Oval

Reproduction
Monoecious

Habitat
Forests and countryside

The gray alder grows in wet, marshy areas. Its long, powerful roots reinforce riverbanks, helping to prevent flooding. Sometimes, its roots reach into the water, providing cover for small fish. Alder roots are also capable of something called "nitrogen fixing," so the tree is sometimes planted to enrich infertile soil. It is not unusual to see "suckers" sprouting from the tree's base.

In winter, the gray alder loses all its leaves, but keeps its strobili—small "cones" housing tiny, winged fruit.

Beavers often use gray alder to build their dams and lodges.

Lifespan
60 to 100 years

Height
15 to 30 feet

Scientific name
Alnus incana

A year in the life...

The gray alder is a **deciduous** tree, shedding its leaves for the winter. It blooms in late winter before the new leaves come out. Its fruit reaches maturity in fall.

Spring | Summer | Fall | Winter

Bark

Gray to brown, with vertical slits and small horizontal streaks.

Not to be confused with...

... the hazel, which has broader and sharper serrated leaves.

Found

The gray alder is common throughout North America, Europe, and Asia.

Observation guide

Northern red oak

A show well worth the wait

Group
Broad-leaved

Shape
Round

Reproduction
Monoecious

Habitat
Forests, countryside, and mountains

Some 600 species of oak can be found throughout the world, most of which are in the Northern Hemisphere. There are two main types of oak tree: white oaks, with round-lobed leaves and acorns that fall to the ground before their first winter; and red oaks, with pointy-lobed leaves and acorns that take two years to mature.

This majestic tree is admired for its gorgeous foliage that turns completely red in fall!

Oaks rely on animals to scatter their acorns. Blue jays and squirrels stock up for the winter by burying them in the ground, with the ones they can't find again going on to become new trees!

Lifespan
~500 years

Height
65 to 100 feet

Scientific name
Quercus rubra

A year in the life...

The northern red oak is a **deciduous** tree, losing its leaves for the winter. It blooms in spring and its acorns take two years to mature.

Spring Summer Fall Winter

Bark

Gray, with deep cracks that form small plates.

Not to be confused with...

... the scarlet oak, whose lobes are more deeply scored.

Found

The northern red oak is common throughout eastern North America and has been introduced into Europe.

Observation guide

A feathered foodie

Among the beautiful fall leaves of the northern red oak, the blue jay can be seen stocking up on acorns. The bird builds up its cache thanks to a pouch under the beak that allows it to carry up to five acorns at a time.

Paper birch

A creamy trunk

Group
Broad-leaved

Shape
Oval

Reproduction
Monoecious

Habitat
Forests, countryside, and mountains

The paper birch has a creamy white bark with black spots that sometimes resemble eyes. What's truly special about the bark is that it peels off in thin strips that look like paper, which Indigenous peoples used to make canoes and roofs for their shelters.

Paper birch seeds keep many bird species coming back for more: from the downy woodpecker to the black-capped chickadee and the white-breasted nuthatch.

In some regions, birch sap is collected in spring to make a delicious honey-flavored syrup.

The paper birch can be very bad for those who have allergies, as it produces a great deal of pollen that travels long distances in the wind.

Lifespan
~120 years

Height
70 to 80 feet

Scientific name
Betula papyrifera

A year in the life...

The paper birch is a **deciduous** tree, shedding its leaves for the winter. Male catkins appear with the arrival of fall and are fully developed by the following spring when female catkins appear before the first leaf.

Spring Summer Fall Winter

Bark

Creamy white, punctuated with black, eye-shaped spots, peeling off in large strips that resemble paper.

Not to be confused with...

... the gray birch, whose leaves taper into a long point.

Found

The paper birch is found throughout Canada and New England and has been introduced into Europe.

Observation guide

Shagbark hickory

No ordinary bark

Group
Broad-leaved

Shape
Oval

Reproduction
Monoecious

Habitat
Forests and countryside

Toward the end of September, nuts from the shagbark hickory break away and fall to the ground. Anyone collecting them for food soon realizes they've got company—squirrels enjoy them too! But the shagbark hickory is in no hurry to share its fruit... it takes about ten years before the first nuts can be harvested, and they won't exactly be plentiful: the tree needs 40 years to reach maximum output.

The shagbark hickory, as its name might suggest, has a highly unusual bark that peels off in long, curly-ended strips. But never judge a tree by its bark... despite the tree's rather shabby appearance, the wood underneath is strong and durable enough to make tool handles. And hickory woodchips are great for adding flavor to any barbecue.

Lifespan
200 to 300 years

Height
60 to 80 feet

Scientific name
Carya ovata

A year in the life...

The shagbark hickory is a **deciduous** tree, losing its leaves for the winter. It blooms in early summer and its nuts are ready for harvest in fall.

Spring Summer Fall Winter

Bark

Brown to gray, pulling away from the trunk in long strips.

Not to be confused with...

... the black walnut, which also has nuts but whose leaves have more leaflets.

Found

Native to eastern North America, the shagbark hickory was introduced into Europe in the 17th century. It grows in rich, moist soil alongside other broad-leaved trees. The tree's northern range ends in southern Quebec.

Observation guide

Sugar maple

A true icon

Group	Shape	Reproduction	Habitat
Broad-leaved	Oval	Monoecious, dioecious	Parks, forests, and countryside

The leaf you see on the Canadian flag is that of the sugar maple, which makes the tree the arboreal emblem of Canada. With such love and respect for the maple tree, it's no wonder Canadians cherish their maple syrup, most of which is produced in Quebec. In fact, the syrup is so yummy it gets shipped all over the world!

The sugar maple is wind pollinated. In spring, sugar maple pollen attracts all kinds of insects. The fruits that follow are samaras that look like tiny propellers, spinning around as they drift off in the wind. Every fall, sidewalks are painted in the beautiful red and orange hues of sugar maples leaves.

Lifespan
250 to 500 years

Height
90 to 120 feet

Scientific name
Acer saccharum

A year in the life...

The sugar maple is a **deciduous** tree, shedding its leaves for the winter. Its blooms appear in spring before the leaves are out. Its fruit matures toward the end of summer.

Spring Summer Fall Winter

Bark

Gray, developing long, vertical ridges that are rigid and erratically shaped.

Not to be confused with...

... the Norway maple, which has similar leaves but more widely angled samaras.

Found

The sugar maple is found only in North America, and is especially common in Quebec.

Observation guide

A syrup to savor

If pancakes or waffles are on the menu, then maple syrup is an absolute must. But getting it to the breakfast table is quite a production!

①

A hole almost half an inch wide is drilled about 2 inches into the trunk of a tree.

②

With the spring thaw, maple sap starts to flow. It's collected with a tap and a pail or long hoses.

④

The syrup is filtered to remove impurities, and then it's finally ready for bottling.

③

To remove the water, the maple sap is boiled at a temperature of 219° Fahrenheit. This process concentrates the sugar levels, and the result is a delicious syrup!

Tamarack

A deciduous conifer

Group
Conifer

Shape
Cone

Reproduction
Monoecious

Habitat
Forests and countryside

The tamarack is an unusual conifer because it drops its needles for the winter! In fall, the needles go from green to a splendid golden yellow. It's no surprise that tamarack forests are popular with hikers.

Tamarack branches are light and thin, and dotted with loads of small, round buds from which rings, or "rosettes," of small, light-green needles emerge. Young, bright red female cones sit alongside mature cones from the year before, and these may stay on the tree for several years.

Woodland birds, such as grouse, love tamaracks for their buds, seeds, and needles. Porcupines like to snack on their bark.

Lifespan
~150 years

Height
50 to 75 feet

Scientific name
Larix laricina

A year in the life...

The tamarack is a **deciduous** tree, shedding its needles for the winter. It blooms in spring and its cones reach maturity the same year, although they can stay on the tree for several years.

Bark

Reddish, cracking into scaly plates with age.

Not to be confused with...

... the bald cypress, who is also a deciduous conifer, but has different needles and cones.

Found

The tamarack is found throughout Canada, the American northeast, and the Great Lakes region.

Observation guide

Common juniper

p. 117

Douglas-fir

p. 121

Redwood

p. 129

Eastern hemlock

p. 125

Subalpine fir

p. 135

Trembling aspen
p. 139

Western redcedar
p. 145

Forests and mountains

Western yew
p. 151

White ash
p. 155

White spruce
p. 161

Common juniper

Berries or cones?

Group
Conifer

Shape
Slender, oval, or round

Reproduction
Dioecious

Habitat
Forests and mountains

The common juniper can cut a variety of figures: low-lying ground cover, round bush, or tall and slender tree. The juniper is at home in the mountains, and its thick, bushy branches make a great home for all sorts of little insects.

Once fertilized, juniper flowers turn into "juniper berries" that can be mistaken for blueberries. Yet, in the botanical sense they aren't even fruit, but mature female cones. That's why they're called "false fruit." Birds enjoy snacking on them but cannot process the seeds... and that's precisely how they're scattered—through bird droppings! Juniper "berries" are used to give some gins their flavor.

Juniper wood has a pleasant smell and anti-moth properties. *Juniperus communis* is too small to be used for lumber, but the eastern redcedar (*Juniperus virginiana*) is sometimes used to make boxes and cabinets.

Lifespan
100 to 200 years

Height
5 to 25 feet

Scientific name
Juniperus communis

A year in the life...

The common juniper is an **evergreen** tree or shrub, which keeps its needles all year.

It blooms in spring and its false fruit take two years to develop.

Bark

Reddish brown and fibrous.

Not to be confused with...

... the western redcedar, which is similarly shaped but has leaves covered in small scales.

Found

The common juniper is found in North America, Europe, and Asia. It can grow at altitudes of over 8000 feet.

Observation guide

Douglas-fir

One-of-a-kind cones

Group	**Shape**	**Reproduction**	**Habitat**
Conifer	Cone	Monoecious	Forests and mountains

Among Canada's native conifers, Douglas-fir is the tallest. It is also native to the United States and Mexico. The superior quality of its timber—a particularly good building material—makes the tree a favorite of the logging industry.

The mature female cones of the Douglas-fir stand out, hanging on the tree with three-pointed, or trifid, bracts which resemble little tridents. But it takes a Douglas-fir 15 years to produce any cones at all.

Like all evergreen trees, Douglas-firs do not lose their foliage all at once, but a little at a time—a cycle that takes five to six years to complete. If you crush a Douglas-fir needle with your fingers, you'll notice a strong, resinous scent with hints of citrus—an odor pleasant to humans but downright repulsive to insects and other plant-eating animals.

Lifespan
~1000 years

Height
100 to 250 feet

Scientific name
Pseudotsuga menziesii

A year in the life...

The Douglas-fir is an **evergreen** tree, keeping its needles all year.

It blooms in spring and its cones reach maturity in fall of the same year.

Why is the common name Douglas-fir hyphenated? Because it's not a true fir! It is similar to other species, and was previously called pine, spruce, hemlock, and true fir. So, in 1867, it was given its own genus—*Pseudotsuga*—which means false hemlock.

Bark

Brown and very thick, with deep cracks that form with age, which expose red-colored trenches.

Not to be confused with...

... the subalpine fir, whose needles bear a strong resemblance, but which has upward-pointing cones, unlike the hanging, or "pendulous," cones of the Douglas-fir.

Found

The Douglas-fir is native to the west coast of the United States and Canada and the mountains of Mexico. It can grow at elevations of up to 6500 feet. It has been introduced into South America, Europe, Australia, New Zealand, and South Africa.

Observation guide

Eastern hemlock

A medicinal tree

Group Conifer	**Shape** Cone	**Reproduction** Monoecious	**Habitat** Forests and mountains

The eastern hemlock bears cones armored with scales that are round and flat, making them look like small roses.

In the past, railroad ties were made from the eastern hemlock's rot-resistant wood and tannin from the bark was extracted to tan leather.

During the European colonization of America, scurvy wreaked havoc everywhere. But thanks to Indigenous peoples' knowledge of the tree's medicinal properties, life-saving remedies were concocted to care for the sick.

Lifespan
~600 years

Height
60 to 70 feet

Scientific name
Tsuga canadensis

A year in the life...

The eastern hemlock is an **evergreen** tree, holding on to its needles all year.

It blooms in spring and its cones reach maturity in fall of the same year.

Bark

Reddish brown, which becomes cracked and scaly with age.

Not to be confused with...

... the white spruce, which has a similar shape but whose needles are quite different: those of the eastern hemlock are arranged flat, while white spruce needles are arranged in a brush-like fashion around the branch.

Found

The eastern hemlock is native to eastern North America, growing at elevations of almost 5000 feet.

Observation guide

Redwood

Reaching dizzying heights!

Group Conifer	**Shape** Cone	**Reproduction** Monoecious	**Habitat** Forests and mountains

This is one tree that's not afraid of heights! The redwood is one of the tallest trees in the world! Its deeply cracked bark makes a perfect home for all sorts of birds, insects, small mammals, and amphibians.

Redwoods need huge amounts of water, which is why their numbers are concentrated in a foggy, humid region near the Northern California coast. They're so tall, their tops just vanish in the mist. Redwoods have a reputation for being fast growers—as much as 3 feet a year.

Despite their enormous size, redwoods can be easily bonsaied. That's right! You can have your very own miniature redwood right in the middle of your living room!

Lifespan
+ 2000 years

Height
200 to 300 feet

Scientific name
Sequoia sempervirens

A year in the life...

The redwood is an **evergreen** tree, keeping its needles all year.

It blooms from mid-winter to spring and its cones reach maturity in fall of the same year.

Bark

Reddish brown, cracked and fibrous.

Not to be confused with...

... the western yew, which has red false fruit (arils) and needles that are flexible, soft, and darker.

Found

The redwood is native to the California coast and Oregon, but has been introduced all over the world. It grows from lowlands to altitudes reaching nearly 3000 feet.

Observation guide

True giants!

California's Redwood National Park is home to the world's tallest tree—a redwood that reaches 379.1 feet into the air!

Subalpine fir

A forest fixture

Group	Shape	Reproduction	Habitat
Conifer	Cone	Monoecious	Forests and mountains

While the cones of the Douglas-fir hang and are found all over the tree, those of the subalpine fir are erect and concentrated at the top. What's more, the cones don't fall to the ground in one piece; instead, they break apart bit by bit as their scales fall off, leaving behind a central spike resembling a candle sitting on the branch. That's why you'll never see a fir cone on the ground!

The tree's needles are arranged in a straight line on the branch, comb-like, and curved slightly upward. The back of each needle is marked with two small white lines.

The subalpine fir is a cousin of the balsam fir and Fraser fir, which are grown commercially as Christmas trees.

Lifespan
~200 years

Height
60 to 100 feet

Scientific name
Abies lasiocarpa

A year in the life...

The subalpine fir is an **evergreen** tree, keeping its needles all year.

It blooms in spring and its cones reach maturity during the same year, but don't fall to the ground whole—instead, little by little, their scales peel away from the inner spike.

Bark

Silvery gray and smooth, dappled with sappy blisters, and cracking with age.

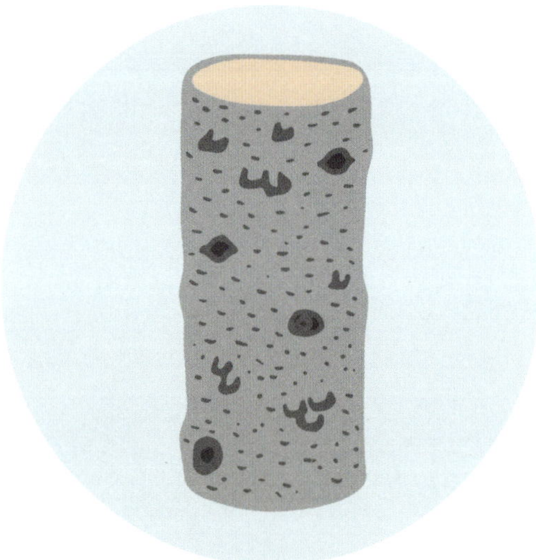

Not to be confused with...

... the Douglas-fir, which has similar needles but whose cones face downward, not upward like those of the subalpine fir.

Found

The subalpine fir is common in western North America and at elevations of over 6500 feet. It often forms the upper treeline in the Rocky Mountains.

Observation guide

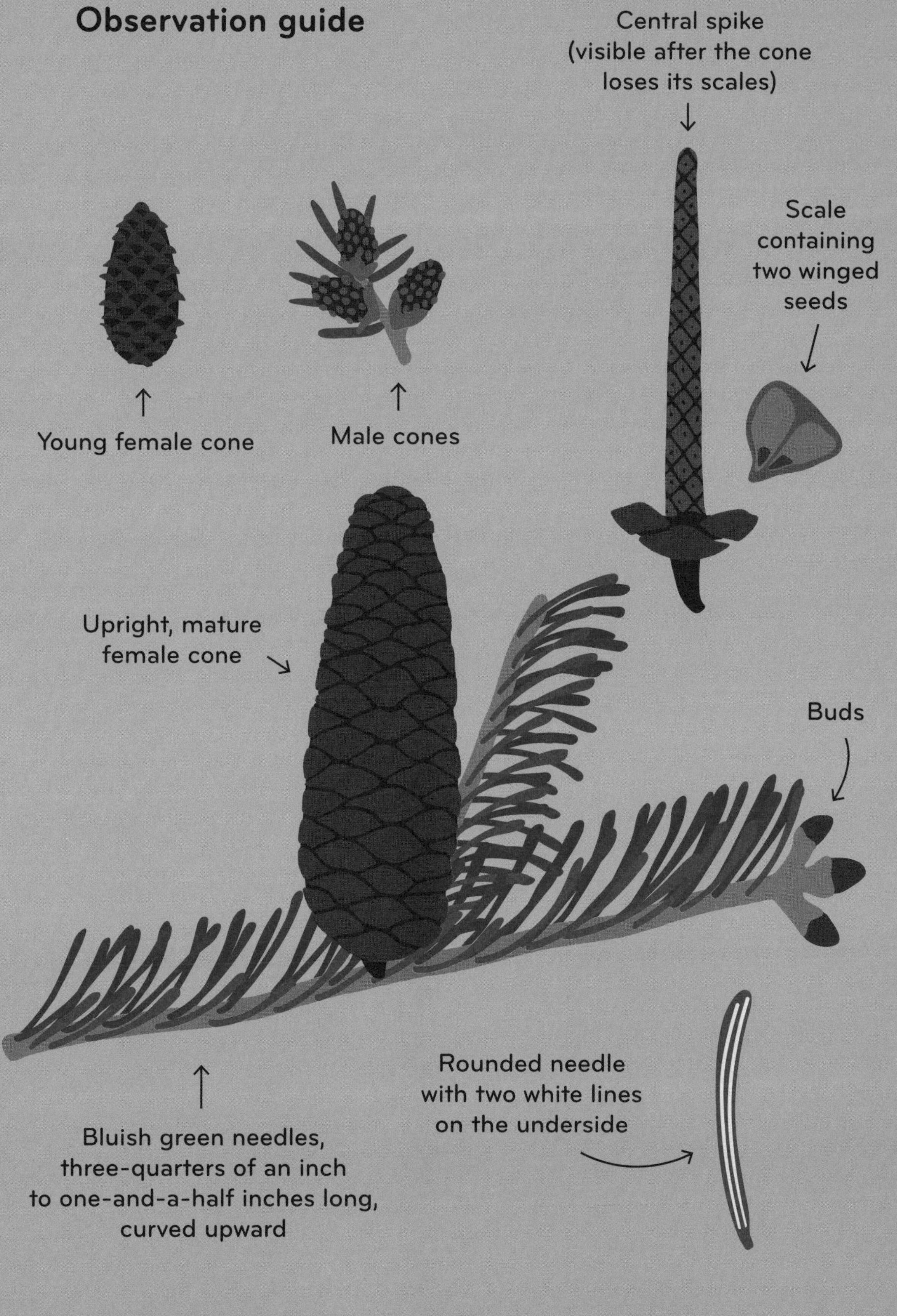

Trembling aspen

A tree that knows how to lay down roots!

Group
Broad-leaved

Shape
Cone, oval

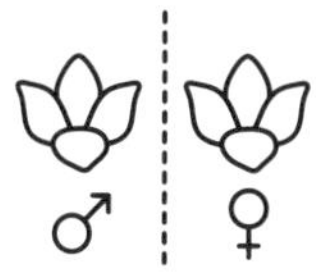

Reproduction
Dioecious

Habitat
Forests, countryside, and mountains

The trembling aspen sports round leaves that taper to a point at the tip and have a flattened stem. The tree's name comes from the fact its leaves tremble with the slightest breeze. The underside of the leaf is not the same color as the topside, so when the tree "trembles," it flickers, as if putting on a pretty light show! In fall, the leaves turn a golden yellow.

The roots of this tree can carve a path through the most compact of soils—they're even capable of cracking concrete sidewalks! Talk about strong! With roots like that, trembling aspens multiply easily—young shoots called "suckers" pop up from the roots, creating clones of the original tree.

Lifespan
~100 years

Height
20 to 50 feet

Scientific name
Populus tremuloides

A year in the life...

The trembling aspen is a **deciduous** tree, dropping its leaves for the winter. It blooms in spring before the leaves appear. The fruiting catkins mature four to six weeks after flowering, and produce wind-dispersed seeds.

Spring

Summer

Fall

Winter

Bark

Waxy, white to greenish in color, which cracks with age.

Not to be confused with...

... the paper birch, which has a similar bark but whose leaves are narrower and pointier.

Found

The trembling aspen has a wide range in North America, but is most abundant in the north, and in mountain ranges of the west.

Observation guide

Talk about an extended family!

Utah is home to the largest living organism in the world: all the trees in "Pando," a 106-acre trembling aspen forest, share the same root system—and the same DNA!

Western redcedar

Scaly leaves

Group
Conifer

Shape
Cone

Reproduction
Monoecious

Habitat
Forests and mountains

Strengthened by roots that fan out at the base of the trunk, the western redcedar is a well-grounded tree. Like many trees in the cypress family, its branches are flat and covered in small, tightly arranged scales. The topside of the branch is dark green, while the underside is green with white markings.

The Cheewhat Giant in British Columbia's Pacific Rim National Park Reserve is the world's largest living western redcedar and one of the biggest trees in the world—a whopping 182 feet tall and 20 feet across!

Western redcedars have been introduced just about everywhere in the world. Sometimes they stand alone in all their glory, or they're grouped with others and trimmed into a hedge.

Lifespan
~800 years

Height
70 to 100 feet

Scientific name
Thuja plicata

A year in the life...

The western redcedar is an **evergreen** tree, keeping its scaly leaves all year.

It blooms in spring and its cones mature in the same year.

Bark

Brown with red or orange hues, fraying and cracking with age.

Not to be confused with...

... the Nootka cypress, which has different cones despite having similar foliage.

Found

The western redcedar is found along the Pacific coast. Native to North America, it has been introduced into Europe, Australia and New Zealand. It can grow at elevations of up to 6500 feet.

Observation guide

Historically important wood

For thousands of years, the western redcedar has been a valuable resource for humans. Indigenous peoples in what is now western Canada used its wood to build boats, baskets, headwear, and totem poles.

Western yew

An understory story

		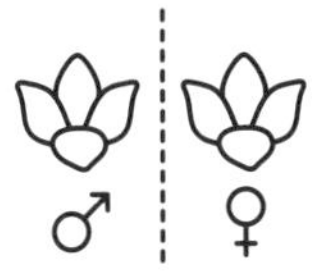	
Group Conifer	**Shape** Cone	**Reproduction** Dioecious	**Habitat** Forests and mountains

The western yew is right at home in the darkness and dampness of the underbrush. In the wild, it tends to be cone-shaped, but it is often trimmed down to a small bush or shaped into a hedge as a property marker. In the past, its supple yet sturdy wood was used to make bows and arrows. Today, the tree's wood is still highly prized by woodworkers and sculptors.

Early in fall, female flowers transform into strange red berries. But these false fruits are "arils." They aren't fruit in the botanical sense, but rather a fleshy casing that grows around the seed—a poisonous seed that is not to go anywhere near your mouth! Only birds can eat them and that's because they poop them out without processing them.

Lifespan
200 to 400 years

Height
20 to 40 feet

Scientific name
Taxus brevifolia

A year in the life...

The western yew is an **evergreen** tree, keeping its needles all year.

It blooms in early spring and its arils ripen toward the end of summer.

Bark

Scaly. The top layer of scales is a purplish brown, peeling away to reveal a layer that is reddish purple or sometimes even bright red.

Not to be confused with...

... the western hemlock, which resembles the western yew but has shorter needles that are a lighter shade of green. Western hemlock branches are brown, while western yew branches are green.

Found

The western yew grows on the west coast of the United States and Canada, as far as Alaska. It can be found at altitudes reaching 6500 feet.

Observation guide

White ash

A sacred tree

Group
Broad-leaved

Shape
Oval

Reproduction
Dioecious

Habitat
Forests, countryside, and mountains

Using its long, powerful roots, the white ash anchors itself deeply into the soil. During winter, the tree stands out because its buds, at the tips of the branches, resemble deer hooves.

Ash lumber is used to make baseball bats. It is the second most popular wood used in the MLB, after the maple.

Unfortunately, ash numbers in North America are declining because of the emerald ash borer. This invasive insect, native to northeastern Asia, most likely arrived in wooden packaging materials in the early 2000s.

Lifespan
~200 years

Height
60 to 70 feet

Scientific name
Fraxinus americana

A year in the life...

The white ash is a **deciduous** tree, dropping its leaves for the winter. It blooms in spring before the leaves come out. The fruit is mature by the fall and remains on the tree all winter.

Spring Summer Fall Winter

Bark

Gray, with a network of ridges.

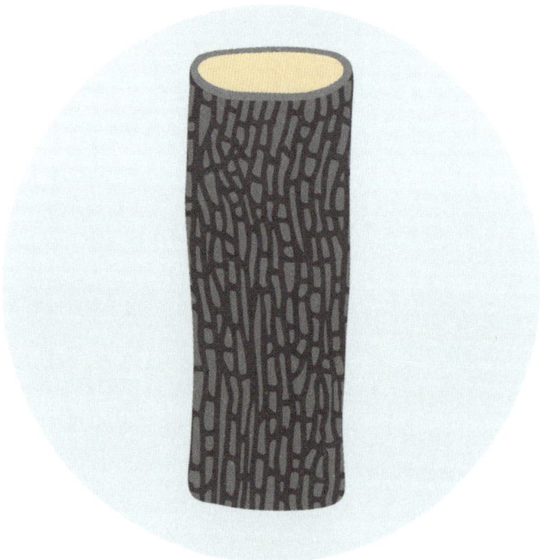

Not to be confused with...

... the black walnut, which has more, and narrower, leaflets. The trees' fruit, however, are nothing alike: the white ash has samaras, while the black walnut has, well, walnuts.

Found

The white ash is found in eastern North America. Europe has different ash species—the most common being *Fraxinus excelsior*.

Observation guide

A fungus with a sweet tooth

As mushroom connoisseurs know, delicious, edible fungi—called morels—grow under ash trees. The tree secretes a delicate sugar from its underground roots, and morels just can't resist.

White spruce

An animal buffet

Group	Shape	Reproduction	Habitat
Conifer	Cone	Monoecious	Forests, countryside and mountains

The white spruce is important to biodiversity because it helps feed numerous mammals, including deer, porcupines, rabbits, and small rodents.

Its wood is composed of long fibers, making it a valuable raw material for paper production.

The white spruce is extremely adaptable, growing happily on riverbanks, lakeside, rocky terrain, and in parks as an ornamental tree. Since it doesn't need a lot of light, it can even grow in dark forests.

The tree has beautiful, bluish green (or "glaucous") needles that form a brush around the branch and emit a powerful, resinous odor.

Lifespan
~200 years

Height
60 to 80 feet

Scientific name
Picea glauca

A year in the life...

The white spruce is an **evergreen** tree, keeping its needles all year.

It blooms in spring. The cones reach maturity after a year but can remain on the tree for two years.

Bark

Dark gray, with small, round scales pulling away from the trunk.

Not to be confused with...

... the subalpine fir, whose needles are curved upward. Its purplish cones also point upward.

Found

The white spruce is found throughout Canada and into Alaska, as well as in the American northeast and states near the Canadian border. It has been introduced into Europe.

Observation guide

Other wondrous trees

of North America and elsewhere

What girth!

California's Sequoia National Park is home to giant sequoias (*Sequoiadendron gigantica*)—some are even big enough to drive through! Giant sequoias and redwoods should not be confused. They are two different species of tree, native to California, that share two common traits—a distinctive bark color, and the ability to grow to incredible heights!

Methuselah

"Methuselah" is a bristlecone pine (*Pinus longaeva*) that is more than 4800 years old! Located in California's Inyo National Forest, it is shaped like a piece of abstract art.

Hey, you're "growing" in the wrong direction!

In order to survive in wet conditions, the bald cypress (*Taxodium distichum*) grows aerial roots, or pneumatophores. These protrude up from the ground to absorb the oxygen the tree needs.

Fabulous flowers

The tulip tree (*Liriodendron tulipifera*) has especially large flowers, whose petals carpet the ground as they wither and fall. It is the tallest eastern hardwood.

Old Tjikko

This Norway spruce (*Picea abies*), located in Sweden, is among the world's oldest trees. It is believed to be 9550 years old!

The Crooked Forest

In Poland, there is a grove of 400 pine trees with strangely bent trunks. Was this the work of humans to make crazy furniture? Is it a marvel of nature? Or perhaps it's something supernatural? No one really knows for sure...

A leafy evergreen

Most broad-leaved trees drop their leaves for winter, but common holly (*Ilex aquifolium*)—which is often used to deck the halls at Christmas—retains its rugged, prickly leaves all year.

Canary Islands dragon tree

If you see an umbrella-shaped crown supported by a maze of branches, you've found a "drago," or Canary Islands dragon tree (*Dracaena draco*)! The bark of this mysterious monocot secretes a reddish resin known as "dragon's blood."

Did you know that palm trees, or monocots, are not really trees? They're actually part of a different botanical family altogether. What's more, they aren't even made of wood!

The red star

The Japanese maple (*Acer palmatum*) has beautiful red leaves that look a lot like stars.

2

Go on, take a good look around!

You can hardly step out your door without seeing a tree. But what do you really know about them? Look at the patterns on their bark or the shape of their leaves. Gather up some cones or look for little winged seeds. There is so, so much to discover!

How to identify a tree

By its shape

- Is the tree slender? Round? Shaped like a cone?
- Is it densely or sparsely leaved?

Subalpine fir

Common apple

Eastern white pine

By its leaves

- How are they shaped?
- Are they simple or compound?
- Is their margin rippled or serrated?
- Are they smooth or hairy?

Sugar maple

Black walnut

Basswood

By its needles

- How are they arranged?
- Do they lie flat on the branch or look like a rosette?
- Are they bundled in groups of two or five?

Douglas-fir

Tamarack

Eastern white pine

By its flowers

- Do they have petals?
- Do they form a catkin?
- Do they look like little cones?

Chokecherry

American hornbeam

Eastern white pine

By its fruit

- Are they fleshy?
- Do they have a protective covering?
- Do they have transparent little wings?

Common apple

American chestnut

American elm

You can even tell what tree it is in winter...

By its bark

- What color is it?
- Is it smooth or notched?
- Do its lines go up and down or side to side?

American sycamore

Western yew

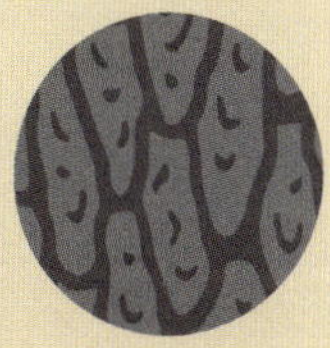

Eastern white pine

By its buds

- Are they oppositely or alternately arranged?
- Are they short and round, or long and pointy?
- Are they smooth or hairy?

Paper birch

American beech

White ash

Leaves and needles

Chokecherry
p. 33

Common apple
p. 37

Gray alder
p. 87

Paper birch
p. 97

American hornbeam
p. 77

American beech
p. 63

American elm
p. 71

Trembling aspen
p. 139

Basswood
p. 23

Southern magnolia
p. 53

American chestnut
p. 67

Ohio buckeye
p. 49

Sugar maple
p. 105

American sycamore
p. 19

Northern red oak
p. 91

Ginkgo
p. 43

White ash
p. 155

Black walnut
p. 29

Shagbark hickory
p. 101

Weeping willow
p. 57

Redwood
p. 129

Western yew
p. 151

Eastern hemlock
p. 125

Subalpine fir
p. 135

White spruce
p. 161

Douglas-fir
p. 121

Common juniper
p. 117

Eastern white pine
p. 83

Tamarack
p. 111

Western redcedar
p. 145

Flowers and young cones

Chokecherry
p. 33

Common apple
p. 37

Southern magnolia
p. 53

Basswood
p. 23

Ohio buckeye
p. 49

American elm
p. 71

Sugar maple
p. 105

American chestnut
p. 67

Northern red oak
p. 91

Ginkgo
p. 43

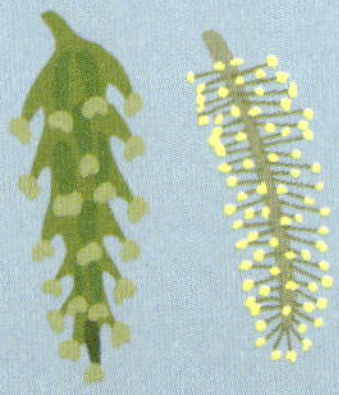

Weeping willow
p. 57

Trembling aspen
p. 139

Black walnut
p. 29

American hornbeam
p. 77

Paper birch
p. 97

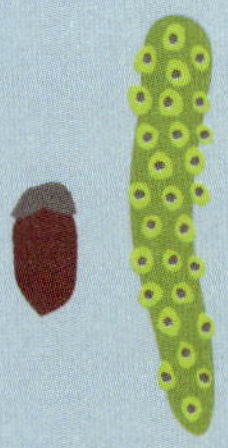

Gray alder
p. 87

On the left ♀

On the right ♂

White ash
p. 155

American beech
p. 63

American sycamore
p. 19

Shagbark hickory
p. 101

White spruce
p. 161

Common juniper
p. 117

Douglas-fir
p. 121

Tamarack
p. 111

Eastern hemlock
p. 125

Western yew
p. 151

Subalpine fir
p. 135

Eastern white pine
p. 83

Redwood
p. 129

Western redcedar
p. 145

Fruit

Chokecherry
p. 33

Common apple
p. 37

Southern magnolia
p. 53

Gray alder
p. 87

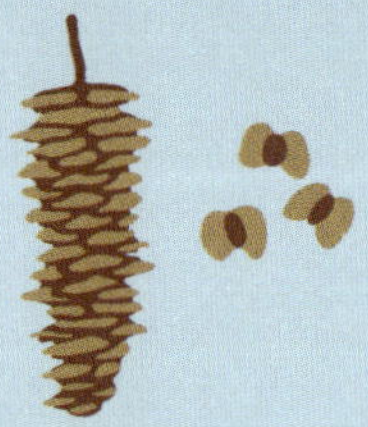

Paper birch
p. 97

Sugar maple
p. 105

White ash
p. 155

American elm
p. 71

American hornbeam
p. 77

American beech
p. 63

American sycamore
p. 19

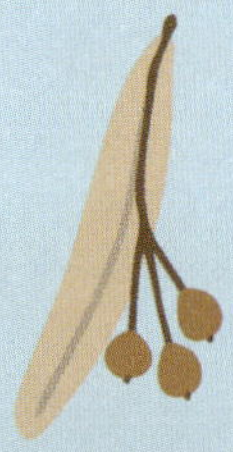

Basswood
p. 23

American chestnut
p. 67

Northern red oak
p. 91

Ohio buckeye
p. 49

Black walnut
p. 29

Shagbark hickory
p. 101

Weeping willow
p. 57

Trembling aspen
p. 139

Cones

Douglas-fir
p. 121

Subalpine fir
p. 135

Eastern white pine
p. 83

Western redcedar
p. 145

Eastern hemlock
p. 125

Tamarack
p. 111

White spruce
p. 161

Redwood
p. 129

Changing with the seasons

Flowers bloom, fruit ripens, leaves change color and fall, and then the cycle starts all over again every spring. With each season, trees undergo a startling transformation!

Spring

Nature awakes from its slumber! Sap once again begins to flow through the branches, and buds start to open. Pretty flowers and tender, pale-green leaves appear. Sometimes, trees such as the cherry, ash, and elm bloom before they even get their leaves.

Summer

This is the season when leaves absorb most of the light they require. This process, known as "photosynthesis," provides trees with sugars that are then carried throughout the trees by their sap. During the summer, trees use their roots to find the water they need to stave off the heat.

Summer is also when colorful fruits, such as plums, peaches, and cherries, make their way to market stands everywhere.

Fall

Days get shorter and darker. The leaves of deciduous trees can no longer produce enough chlorophyll, a green pigment that is necessary for photosynthesis to occur. And, so, the green in the leaves gives way to other pigments ranging from yellow to red. The leaves slowly die and then fall to the ground, where they may continue to help by protecting the roots.

With evergreen trees, old needles also end up on the ground, but in much smaller numbers. Depending on the species, a conifer's entire foliage is replaced every three to five years.

Winter

The sap in deciduous trees stops flowing and they lose all their leaves. This is a vital process for trees because any water in the sap could freeze and cause them to die. With conifers, on the other hand, the needles are cold-resistant thanks to their waxy texture.

Trees that shed their leaves go into a state of "dormancy"—life goes on, but at a slower pace, with their roots still absorbing the nutrients they need to survive. Their survival also depends on the sugars—a natural antifreeze—that accumulates in their wood during the warmer months.

Bark—a tree's armor

A tree's bark shields it against all forms of attack: insects, animals, disease, or extreme temperatures.

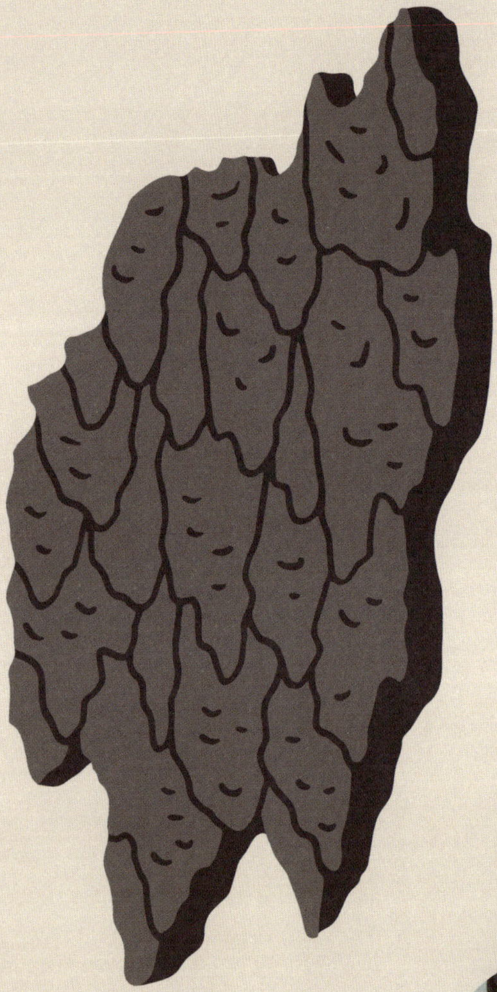

Weird markings

When bark has white or green spots on it, it's usually lichen or moss. These feed off the minerals trickling down a tree's bark, which is why studying lichen allows us to better understand air-pollution levels.

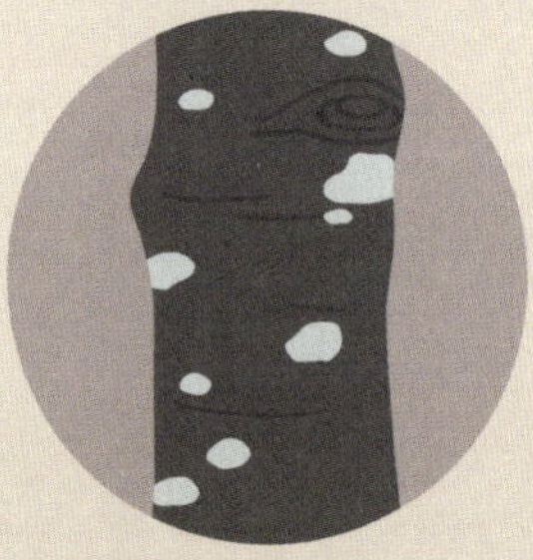

Roots—a tree's anchor

Roots allow trees to withstand powerful winds. Underground, they extract the water and nutrients trees need to survive, even during winter.

Lateral root system

These roots spread out horizontally to cover a large area, without penetrating too deep into the soil. Examples include the roots of the paper birch, sugar maple, and white ash.

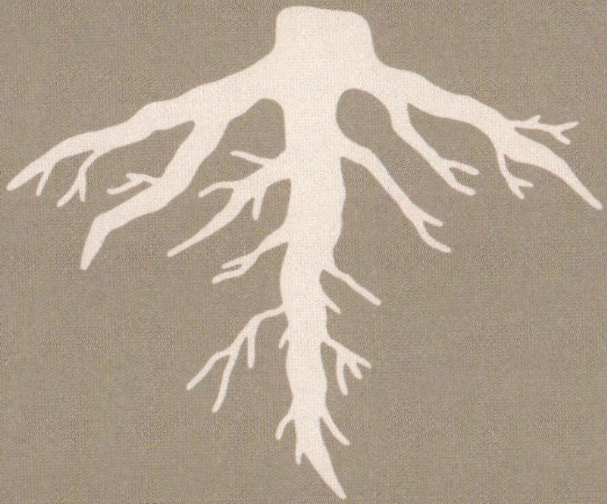

Taproot system

The dominant root pushes down deep into the soil and is surrounded by other, finer roots. The American hornbeam, eastern white pine, shagbark hickory, and black walnut have this type of root.

Heart root system

These roots all start from the same point, shooting out in every direction to form a system resembling a heart or triangle. The northern red oak, American sycamore, and basswood all have this sort of root system.

3

The life of trees

They might seem to just stand there, but trees are actually quite busy! They are growing new roots, absorbing light, fending off parasites, growing taller, reproducing, and coexisting with other plant and animal species.

Some trees are planted in parks where they stand majestically for hundreds of years, while others are sent to the sawmill. Some thrive, to be admired, while others still are threatened with extinction… one thing's for sure—every tree has a story!

The life of a tree

The lifecycle of a black walnut

1. The nut opens up, and a seed sprouts and takes root.
2. A seedling develops, getting its first leaves.
3. Buds appear.
4. The next year, the buds become branches and leaves, with flowers appearing after several years.
5. The flowers pollinate one another, and reproduction occurs.
6. Female flowers turn into fruit.
7. The fruit falls to the ground, where seeds sprout the following year!

Reproduction

Animals can search for a mate but trees are stationary, so they need to be a little more creative!

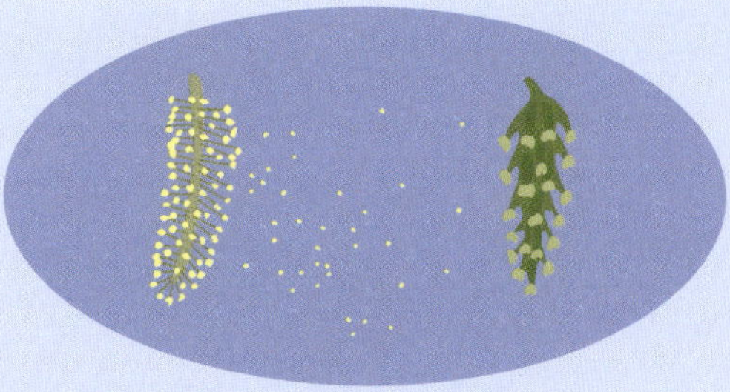

Wind

The wind blows pollen from male flowers to female flowers. Some trees have winged seeds that also rely on the wind to travel.

Animals

Animals feed on nuts and fruits, and their movement helps disperse seeds.

Suckers

Young sprouts called "suckers" grow from tree roots and are clones of the mother tree.

Grafting

Grafting is a technique developed by humans. It consists of splicing the branch of one tree onto another variety or even species. For example, an apricot branch can be grafted onto a plum tree!

Guessing a tree's age

Sun exposure, soil quality, and even elevation are factors that determine a tree's growth rate. Still, there are a few ways to estimate a tree's age.

Counting its rings

In the right conditions, trees grow a new ring every year. With a little patience, you can count them one by one!

Measuring its circumference

Try the following equation to work out a tree's approximate age:

1. With a measuring tape, measure the circumference of the trunk (in inches) about 4.5 feet above the ground.
2. Divide this number by pi (3.14) to get the diameter.
3. Multiply the diameter by a growth factor specific to each species of tree.

For the black walnut, for example:
75 inches ÷ 3.14 × 4.5 = 107 years old

Growth factor examples:
2 for poplars
3 for basswoods
4 for northern red oaks and elms
4.5 for black walnuts
5 for sugar maples

Counting its stories

Conifers add a new layer of branches or whorls every year. If a tree is not too tall or bushy, you can determine its age by counting the number of stories, although it isn't always easy!

Can you guess how old this tamarack is?

Home to all sorts of creatures

1. Ants use fallen twigs to build their colony.
2. A squirrel finds a safe haven—and food too!
3. A caterpillar munches on leaves.
4. A red fox settles in for a nap in its den under the roots.
5. A beaver uses branches to build a dam.
6. Fungi grow on the bark.
7. Earthworms loosen the soil, bringing nutrients to the roots.
8. A longhorn beetle feeds on decaying wood.
9. A deer savors any leaf within reach.
10. A white-breasted nuthatch builds its nest in a hollow, eating any seeds and insects it can find.
11. Voles munch on roots beneath the soil.

The benefits of having trees around

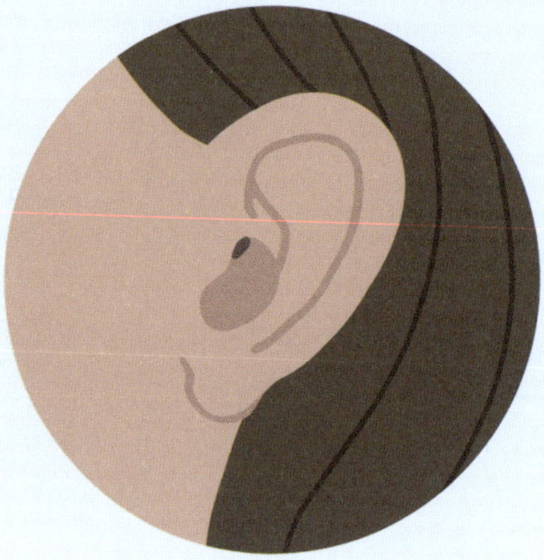

They reduce noise pollution

They're a precious food source

They provide wood for making so many things

They give off oxygen and clean the air

They give shade
and cool the air

They beautify
our cities and parks

They protect us from
avalanches and landslides

They're used to make
medicines

Wood, cardboard, paper...

... essential materials that come from trees!

Species at risk

The outlook is not at all good: globally, 30% of tree species are threatened with extinction. Yet, ecosystems cannot function properly without them. The main causes are pest insects and parasitic fungi, but humans are equally to blame because of deforestation, intensive agriculture, and climate change.

1. American chestnut

These trees are threatened by a fungus: chestnut blight. In just 30 years, 99% of American chestnut trees in the United States were wiped out. Hybrids are being developed to keep the species alive.

2. Ash

For years now, ashes have been threatened by the emerald ash borer, a tiny insect that accidentally hitched a ride to America in shipping crates. Its larvae dig a course under the bark, blocking the flow of sap. Considerable effort has gone into slowing the death of thousands of ashes in the American east.

3. Elm

Since the middle of last century, elms have been plagued by Dutch elm disease, a fungus that is spread by an insect, the elm bark beetle. Sap flows poorly in infected trees, and the tunnels dug by the insect are visible on the trunks.

4. Redwood

Despite their popularity and symbolic importance in the United States, redwood (and giant sequoia) populations are threatened due to excessive logging in the past. Plus, their natural range is limited and their preferred foggy habitat may not be stable in a warming climate.

①
②
③
④

What can we do to help trees?

Humans have a big role to play in protecting trees. Here are a few simple things you can do to help.

Use reusable materials instead of paper whenever possible

Take part in activities that help the forest

Respect the forest by adopting a "carry in-carry out" rule

Reduce your environmental footprint to fight climate change

Recycle paper and cardboard

Don't waste food and use biodegradable products

Buy second-hand furniture

ARBORAMA
The Marvelous World of Trees

Educator's Guide

What makes trees unique in the plant world? How can we learn more about the ways trees grow and how trees help people and other creatures? What can we do to protect trees? Let's find out!

Educator's Guide
by Christina Moorehead
and Izzy Krause

OBSERVE

Tree teachers

This book is filled with amazing illustrations of trees. How do the illustrations compare with real, living trees? Go to a place where trees are growing and explore the trees with your senses of touch, sight, hearing, and smell (but not taste, unless it is an actual fruit tree!). Write/draw what you can learn from the book that you can't learn from the living tree. Then write/draw what you can learn about the living tree that you cannot learn from the book.

Tree-cosystems

Among the many ways trees support the ecosystem around them, trees provide food and shelter for other living creatures. Go to a place where trees are growing and using only your senses of sight and hearing, see if you can find other living creatures—large and small—that depend on trees to stay alive and healthy.

EXPLORE

Climate-savers

Trees play a big part in helping the Earth's climate stay at a healthy temperature for living things. But how? Explore the powers of plants by getting two clean, empty glass pickle jars and putting a small potted plant in one, and leaving the other jar empty. Put both jars in a sunny window. Put a thermometer in each jar and record the temperatures every day.

Ring around the years

How old are the trees that you see around your neighborhood or city? Compared to smaller plants, trees can live an amazingly long time. Apple trees can live over 100 years. Oak trees can live over 500 years. Some redwood trees can live up to 2000 years! But how do we know the ages of trees? We count the rings. Once a tree has died, people cut a section across the trunk. Inside are rings—each ring stands for one year of age. Get some pieces of lumber—from your house or from a home supply shop, or ask a tree maintenance company if they can give you some tree sections after they cut down a tree—and then start counting! Do you notice any differences between rings? How are the rings in the center different from the rings closer to the outside?

Tree-stories

Trees help humans and animals in many ways. Choose one tree that you observed using your senses, and write a story about the many different ways living creatures use the tree. How might members of your community benefit from the tree? Do animals use the tree? If it's a warm day, you could even sit underneath the tree as you write your story—for shade AND inspiration!

PROTECT

Replant a forest

There are many forests that have lost trees due to storms, drought, and other natural disasters. These forests can be replanted—if people choose to help! You can help by hosting a FUNDRAISER at your school or in your community. The money you earn can be donated to help organizations such as The Arbor Day Foundation, which replants trees in forests across the country.

Educate others

Most people know that trees are important, but do they know why? Take action by teaching others about the many ways trees help keep the environment, other creatures, and people healthy and alive! You can create tree-focused posters to display in public spaces (with permission!), create a zine, or make a video or other informative art piece that shows the world exactly why trees are important to us all.

Recycled paper art

Have you ever noticed how many pieces of paper get thrown away? Instead of tossing your paper scraps, finished worksheets, or art drafts away, you can we turn that paper into more art! Use a box to collect all of your used pieces of paper and create a cut or torn paper collage. You can also cut the paper into squares and make recycled paper origami. You can even make new paper from the used paper by tearing it into very small pieces, soaking it in water, and then pressing it flat! What other ways can you think of to creatively reuse paper?

About the author

My name is Lisa Voisard and I was born in Lausanne, Switzerland, in 1992. As a graphic artist, illustrator, and musician, I have always had a need to create, and through my creations I have found countless ways to express myself!

For me, having knowledge of the things around me is very important—every leaf and every twig has a secret story to tell, and it's my job to share them!

Arborama will appeal to children, but I hope adults enjoy it, too, as a way to deepen their understanding of nature.

Let's take care of our planet's biodiversity, and let's also learn to work with our planet, not against it. Earth is our home, and it needs some TLC.

Thank you...

Shagbark hickory

To everyone at Helvetiq, for your faith in me and being by my side to help create and promote *Arborama*.

To Andrée Hallé for adapting the book for an American audience and to Paul D. Henne for reviewing it.

To Malik Beytrison, who was an invaluable source of support. I discovered so many things during our outings. To my parents and my sister, for steadfastly supporting me on all my adventures.

To trees... if it weren't for you, we wouldn't have books!

Index